ANAPHORA

ANAPHORA

Kevin Goodan

Alice James Books
Farmington, Maine
alicejamesbooks.org

10 9 8 7 6 5 4 3 2 1

Alice James Books are published by Alice James Poetry Cooperative, Inc., an affiliate of the University of Maine at Farmington.

Alice James Books
114 Prescott Street
Farmington, ME 04938
www.alicejamesbooks.org

Library of Congress Cataloging-in-Publication Data

Names: Goodan, Kevin, 1969- author.
Title: Anaphora / Kevin Goodan.
Description: Farmington, ME : Alice James Books, [2018]
Identifiers: LCCN 2018020531 (print) | LCCN 2018023167 (ebook) | ISBN
   9781948579520 (eBook) | ISBN 9781938584961 (paperback : alk. paper)
Subjects: | BISAC: POETRY / General.
Classification: LCC PS3607.O563 (ebook) | LCC PS3607.O563 A63 2018 (print) |
   DDC 813/.6--dc23
LC record available at https://lccn.loc.gov/2018020531

Alice James Books gratefully acknowledges support from individual donors, private foundations, the University of Maine at Farmington, the National Endowment for the Arts, and the Amazon Literary Partnership.

Cover art: "RA" by Andrew McIntosh

CONTENTS

Acknowledgments

Some of these poems were published as an online chapbook by Connotation Press: An Online Artifact in their A Poetry Congeries column.

For Jimmy who hung himself
For Kevin who hung himself
For Garcia who hung himself

We who have our flourishings
our little moments of shine
here, where the roaring is
the purge of what is granted
when heat is the translation
of some common god, when we
sway grateful for flame
in the way we yearn to hold
it all, feel it all, good
because I am something that will
burn in the violence of the
beginning of tomorrow
which embers down the home
we are calling to it is
November the bright book says
we belong

November the bright book
we are calling to burns
because I am the in *the* violence
of tomorrow the translations
sway here some common god grateful
for the purge beginning
the embers how clean
we shine in the roaring
how sweet home burns

November codename for belong
Jimmy singing fuck fuck your dog
in the flourishing because god
is beginning tomorrow common ember
the bright book translation
Houdini says Rosabelle believe
by the watertower in the way
we yearn to roar the violence
and Jimmy laughing, dead

If we flourish for some common god
then who is grateful for home
the translation of fuck your dog
into tomorrow we sway the heat
into shine we are calling I am
the common belong a moment
beginning in the way violence begins
little and granted Joe Grady calling
from the bright book swaying flame

Joe Grady Houdini fuck your dog
Rosabelle play to the burn
which is flourishing codename
Watertower this is November
Echo Charlie Kilo translation
hang/we are calling to
tomorrow believe in sway
the bright book says gone

The bright book says Joe Grady dead
Houdini fucks to believe
codename moment codename flourish
November is what we are calling to
Echo Charlie what does Kilo say
to purge the god of watchtowers
codename tomorrow the heat of
translation Rosabelle sways
feels it all good grateful roaring
I am something that will belong

For Jimmy who hung himself
For Kevin who hung himself
For Garcia who hung himself

For Jimmy who hung himself
For Kevin who hung himself
For Garcia who hung himself

I am flourishing
Joe Grady fucks Houdini
Rosabelle Charlie and dogs
we are dead translations
grateful gods all violence
and flame the common moment
sway and we sway fuck
we Echo and the callsigns
November tomorrow Kilo
it is you we are calling to
says the book believe
burning on the watertower

A can of Skoal
and a pocket of Charlie
we burn beneath the watertower
Rosabelle fucks it all
with a violence in the weeds
because I am Houdini
tomorrow believe the shine
when you see it Joe
when what you are granted
is home

Sway November watertower bright
where Rosabelle believed
fuck Joe Grady fuck your dog
dead as the Houdini you rode in on
goodbye Scott goodbye Doug
how clean it all how sweet it all
burns in the callsign Kilo
where my cousin Jimmy hangs
yearning for the word: belong
can't pick the locks goodbye
Harry the book the flames bid
singing fuck singing home
see my Houdini flies

Harry Houdini picks the locks
of death goodbye Rose goodbye
Belle cousin Jimmy hangs Echo
has a kilo of fuck-dog something
I am yearning sweet violence
burns the common calling home
how clean it all shines
feel it all good the bright
book belongs to watertower god
who will sway November tomorrow

Dropzone November this is Houdini
believe Joe Grady picks the locks
that echo tomorrow dog where Jimmy
belongs god not no ligature flame
that will burn because we roar
with violence granted we fuck and hang
because we are so good I am Charlie
I am Rosabelle callsign Kilo goodbye
someone cut my cousin down please
goodbye goodbye cut him the fuck down

Hey Joe got some Skoal

some shine and a callsign

there's too much heat

come back tomorrow I am

what are you doing writing a book

bright real bright fuck

now you got some embers in your shorts

translate that on the watertower

that's not where we belong

because everybody picks on Houdini

even Rosabelle believe it

not Echo maybe Charlie

what's that smell who's burning

God you keep spitting on my boot

what's you gonna do call your momma

come on Joe come on Jimmy

let's get some rope I bet

he won't even weigh a kilo

when we're done I think he's

got a yearning to sway anyhow

Cut my cousin down
Joe Grady's dead
Jimmy get rid of that earring
we who sway in the dropzone
chromatic blue of hanging
the flourishing moment
codename grateful calling to
something I can hold something
common of the moment that will
echo our belief here
at the watertower where we
purge tomorrow of its shine

[chorus]

Echo November we are over
the dropzone over roger that
prepare to hang Jimmy
just like Houdini all locks
and earrings a pinch
of Skoal goodbye Charlie Kilo
hello flame I sway

Here Garcia hangs Kevin hangs
and Jimmy half-breed chromatic
picking the rope that belongs to
Houdini roaring through locks
I am something good translate me
grateful something common little
Joe Grady flourishing before violence
granted by embers oh home
three hang we all hang tomorrow

Because Jimmy did I am
don't you stop me Joe
let's meet at the watertower
I'll bring flame there's a lot
of similarities between hanging
and drowning you flail and blue
I need Skoal if we're going to
I need god what he says
it's all callsign and codename
feel it there ain't no dropzone
where we belong only shine
we'll be echo beginning tomorrow

Day-shine ligature god
these are the callsigns
the translations of here
the common flame swaying
for the beginning we are
calling to November I am
violence the bright book
says chromatic like Jimmy
like Joe Grady shot dead
here the dropzone I can't
clean it all not even then
I feel all the embers down
where the roaring is home

We pick the locks purge the home
Joe Grady is stumbling after
Jimmy says half-breed wants a pulaski
my cousin's tired of hanging
Houdini did it we can do it
Rosabelle will never believe
we cut the rope and burn the rope
say grateful flames to god
because I am something that will
hold it all feel it all
the heat of our common yearning
there is no codename never callsign
the bright book says we dead

Slipknots and chicken pox
and Little Lamb cheats Divy
in her sway above the tower
who else do we know that'll shine
goodbye Joe goodbye Jimmy half-
breed goodbye into the violence
of our callsign: November
Echo Charlie Kilo: codename
Hang the Fucking Dog

[chorus]

Dropzone Fuck come in over
Fuck can you read me over
roger that dog all things shine
proceed to November god
our flourishings are little
because of home that belongs
in tomorrow the bright book
sways in the zone we yearn
we flame we ember the Echo
believe little lambs feel all
the violence I am

Permutations of Houdini
as callsigns for god for all
that slips the knot of tomorrow
here no shine feel the goodbye
burn Jimmy half-breed hanging
Joe Grady dead not November
who holds a pulaski I am
grateful for the echo of believe
sway the watertower pick
no locks for once and all belong

Dear Annette I burned your hair
should've seen the shine
I picked your lock
you slobbed Joe's cock
I dream-fucked that plump behind
once you were blonde
and kind of pudgy-cute
but you gave us all pox
downed the whole keg
and moved your ass to Butte

For Jimmy who hung himself
For Kevin who hung himself
For Garcia who hung himself

For Jimmy who hung himself
For Kevin who hung himself
For Garcia who hung himself

For Jimmy who hung himself
For Kevin who hung himself
For Garcia who hung himself

We listened to the station's
callsign: Kilo Echo Rat Rat
said Doug Bell found
blue in the pond said
Jimmy found blue in the noose
spastic like Houdini
picking the locks of god
so he ain't here to see
us flourish good said Rose
I believe November
had something to do with it
Joe Grady said he never did
belong Annette said someone
burned my hair then the air
just dropped I hear
the marshall is towing tonight

I am the marshall I am
flame that embers your house
Jimmy said Annette plump
and fucking chromatic
why do the pudgy shine
Joe holds rope by the hair
says we should call by name
all we feel that's good
we tow Doug to the watertower bell
clanging when we're empty of god

Give us a callsign and
we'll give you my dead over
Charlie bells makes
flames believe
any name that belongs
to what Marshall holds
here between embers
of ligature chromatic

Couldn't watch the show
because of the flames
Mary an ember inside them
we towed Dougie down
to where some gods hang out
Jimmy said that's how
you find him ass in the air
just pulling that hair
Rose spurring her heels
beside them

Home from town
the struggle
to believe swaying
what I am
stoking the fire
my eye seeps like
Joe Grady's wound
eternal I let
my arms hang sore
from packing Jimmy
all these twenty years
always the lights
of the watertower
bright like the book
of codes I write
everybody's name in

A loop of rope
a watertower blue
that's how cousin yearns it
we read for signs
November translates
of violence into purge
the book at home says
Jimmy is flourishing
every flame needs to belong
to shine but our people
are common hang on god
know what roaring is
but Jimmy but I we
feel it ember not burn
I'd give him Rose
because he knows
how little moments
are granted

We gather to the flame
and some get burned
Jimmy's shoes are swaying
from the catwalk
slick with rain chromatic
they say our town is
flourishing but Joe Grady
says it's November
and everyone is calling home
we listen to the gravel pit
roar for the common good
we all hold hands and feel it
embers we say because we know
what it's like to belong

We fuck the gods
we crush chromatic
Jimmy cuts the ropes
grateful we are calling
the signs for home
but when we yearn
we ember terrible
everyone good with holes
this November it was
Joe Grady and Mary and Rose
whose next Houdini
says Jimmy am I gonna
make your flesh shine?

When we burned the ligature
we watched the blue flames hang
Jimmy swayed with them
in the purge of windy flourishes
down to something we call
home and you call ember
the reader Annette said
ain't gonna believe nothing
in your book but the roaring

If you get blue I get
chromatic says Jimmy
to Joe who's fucking
my cousin Annette was
there with her burned
off hair yearning for
the watertower a flamed-
out god grateful to be
embered swaying without
the shine you'll have
your moment to-morrow
says Doug roping down
this is not a place
where we belong
not since the beginning
of November go home

Quick pick the lock Houdini
Jimmy says hurry says Annette
I gots to pee Joe is working
the tumblers like some thieving
god but we're trying to get back
to where we belong Jimmy nips
a sip of shine says he don't
have to see to feel it all
says my breath is flame
hand me the rope Grady says
cause I feel a yearning coming on
for Rosabelle and one way
or another I'm gonna get me
a bite of her sweet ass

Jimmy Joe and god
all hang (little houdinis)
from the watertower
blue as the inside of flames
everywhere else the day shines
I feel it am grateful for
November a moment of
summer's echo purging
the common gray
at night we're all callsign
and violence Charlie says
we'll be dead tomorrow
because of sin or maybe
the Soviets I say we are here
for a while we are just
beginning he smiles says
he can hear the roaring

My cousin ain't no Belle
I said he's just a flame
likes a good rose I said
Jimmy took out his knife
cut a hunk of rope said
you can't get out of this one
Houdini someone's gonna pay
tomorrow I can feel it good
well I said beginning to ember
violence is how we belong
when we have no home
quit your roaring he said
here is where I flourish
but your cousin is gonna sway

My cousin Jimmy Joe Grady
Annette and Doug codenames
haunts and whispers of the thing
we grant because I yearn
to belong to them some violent
and common home I'm calling to
because I feel it shining all the way
from tomorrow where I sway
grateful for the burn

The marshall's at the tower
studying flames Jimmy danced
called it his rope dance of
love Mary said all he wanted
was to fuck shouldn't any boy
at least be given that embers
smashed chromatic beneath
a Buick Joe Grady says
tonight we bomb him home
taps his hip says give them
a taste of Rose ammo up
Dougie says we got blue dogs
coming round can't hang here
I'm already on the books

They don't breed them like they used to
Marshall says putting his claw around
the shine all the children chromatic
spotless for every tomorrow they was
good kids never roaring just yearning
to be something grateful like I am
now all the violence beginning every-
body leaving their homes in embers
I think we could use a proper purge
hang them all from the watertower
like the bright book says that will
will learn them what the fuck maybe
they'll find god and we need to start
with that little flame Jimmy, dawg

Joe Grady said he fucked a dog
below the watertower with a
garden hose up its ass he said
and then I turned it on
till water shot out its mouth
Mary wanted to hang him
Rose didn't believe because she took
a shine to him Jimmy said you
must sit at home and dream this
violence go hang yourself Joe
said so he did it was November
we were supposed to read our books

For Jimmy who hung himself

For Kevin who hung himself

For Garcia who hung himself

For Jimmy who hung himself

For Kevin who hung himself

For Garcia who hung himself

For Jimmy who hung himself

For Kevin who hung himself

For Garcia who hung himself

For Jimmy who hung himself

For Kevin who hung himself

For Garcia who hung himself

For Jimmy who hung himself

For Kevin who hung himself

For Garcia who hung himself

For Jimmy who hung himself
For Kevin who hung himself
For Garcia who hung himself

For Jimmy who hung himself
For Kevin who hung himself
For Garcia who hung himself

For Jimmy who hung himself
For Kevin who hung himself
For Garcia who hung himself

For Jimmy who hung himself
For Kevin who hung himself
For Garcia who hung himself

For Jimmy who hung himself
For Kevin who hung himself
For Garcia who hung himself

For Jimmy who hung himself
For Kevin who hung himself
For Garcia who hung himself

For Jimmy who hung himself

For Kevin who hung himself

For Garcia who hung himself

For Jimmy who hung himself

For Kevin who hung himself

For Garcia who hung himself

For Jimmy who hung himself

For Kevin who hung himself

You can't drag me back
to that watertower after
what Joe Grady did Jimmy
said Oh fuck said Mary
quit being such a flame
Rose just wants to take
you home either
you or Dougie or Marshall
you think this is my calling
Jimmy said because I am
something that will sway
she wants to make your
little pecker shine boy
it's November too cold
to feel it all good god
said Mary you don't know
what you are being granted
do you need a translator
or something Oh no Oh no
said Rose Joe Grady just
got shot he's dead dead

We walk down to the IGA
buy a pack of baloney
walk back to the watertower
waiting for the moment
Mrs. Miele said the world
would end once and for all
the moment comes/it goes
we're eating baloney
that bitch doesn't know shit
I say and sure as hell
can't teach dog-dicks
Jimmy says not a word
what do you think it will
be like all flame and ember
I ask Jimmy smiles says
help me burn the end of this
here rope

I need a callsign says Jimmy
so you know it's me trying
to get in touch I might be
out of range for a while
how about *Fuck Dog* I say
and he says something official
like for airplanes and rocket ships
what about Marshall he says
and I say Jimmy you ain't never
going that far this is where
you and I belong home he says
making a loop of rope and
throwing it over a beam here
he says get up on that chair
and let's test this all out

Let all the broke-dicks hang
Mary said pulling her jeans
back on there's got to be
another way said Doug you
are one of them said Rose
I'm the one that drowned
said Doug and Jimmy everyone
knows how tight that rope was
his head almost popped clean off
what a sight that would be
said Mary that beautiful head
rolling on the ground singing
blue songs in that quailing voice
about fucking my sweet ass

Hey Dougie let's go swimming down
in the old gravel pond can't right now
why because I'm dead well if you
change your mind that's where we'll be
just fucking around hanging out
you're forgetting something real
important you dumb bastard I drowned

If Jimmy hangs today
we're all screwed says Mary
believe it says Annette
adjusting her glittery garter
he's everybody's flame says
Joe Grady good god says
Mary don't get soppy remember
what he did at the watertower
before or after the marshall
shined his light what a night
says Annette who knew screwing
could be so violent bunch of
dogs says Joe if Jimmy hangs
we all deserve it

What's the matter Annette
got a dick stuck in your craw
says Jimmy shining the light
around the watertower you know
the marshall's towing tonight
don't you Joe/Joe stays mum
everybody hears the click of the
gun goodnight Joe goodnight Belle
goodnight Jimmy goodbye burn

The dead belong to the watertower
a higher place to hang with no
codename with no callsign each
of them a blue flame even the
marshall nods as he tows tonight
into tomorrow the common god he is
burning with the violence no one
can translate into belief but the
pattering November rain

Some die and some
want to die those
are the facts
Jimmy says tossing
the rope from the
watertower none of
us are but a flame
fuck off says Mary
god's on my side
not if you keep
screwing those breeds
says Jimmy shut up
says Annette you're
half a one Jimmy
I say which half
you gonna hang?

Walking in the snow
Jimmy burning in my head
hallelujah we all believe
in a watertower its light
could save us you can't
Houdini the past Joe Grady
said no matter where you
hang was nothing
but a fool for November
said Rose kicking the rope
it's not like we were brothers I said only
cousins second ones at that
I put my hands in the snow
Jimmy burns my head

Jimmy said everybody
hangs in hell so why not
get a head start?
Fuck Jimmy said Mary you
really know how to lift
a party Jimmy tied the knot said
I'll see you all at the
watertower

This is not November Jimmy said
this is god and he's fucking us over
he wipes the shine from his face
wimpers is silent you me
said Joe we should climb that tower
shoot flaming arrows at his ass
that would get his attention you can't
burn heaven stupid said Mary but you
can torch the hair of Annette
you skanks need to jump back Jimmy
said I'm gonna do my rope dance
tonight he said you and I
shall twirl in the flames of paradise

Hang the rich Joe Grady said
on the porch of his daddy's trailer
then he stood up and said we should
walk the levee and the only one
was around the sewer lagoon
so we walked it he spat in the stench
and said when I die it's gonna be
in a really small town not no fucking
city he scuffed the dirt with his boot
it was his birthday he squinted
said I ain't gonna die a virgin he pulled at the tag
of his tee shirt scratched the pocket
above his heart we listened to the sounds
of the mill horn closing the shift
he kept itching the pocket said
it feels like a flame in there
let's go shoot some dogs he said
when he died it was in a parking lot
of the Dew-drop Inn a fight
over the woman he was fucking
I was living in a city

59

Jimmy says fuck
the marshall's towing tonight
and the Buick loaded up
with shine Blue-Flame-of-God
we call it codename for the burn
in the heart Joe Grady gets
knocking some back knocking some
ass down the car ain't got no heater and it's
November but it's clean running
and high geared which translates into
speed and when it goes to blackout
you can't even see it from
the watertower but you hear
the cutouts open all the way
to the river dammit says Jimmy
running out the door they done
already hauled it

What do you do Jimmy
when the voices get loud
I asked he said I go
to the watertower and let
the voices burn but I'm
scared of heights I said
you don't have to climb it
you can just stand there
and take it all in or
close your eyes and stand
in the lights sometimes
you can see right through
yourself you can see
that you're only a callsign
a name and nothing more
what do you do if that
doesn't work I asked
he said I climb the tower
are you scared of heights
I asked sure he said
but it doesn't matter why
I asked because I'm already
dead you moron

We got the posi-track
the big block loping
and Grady crashing his hand
through the gears
some call this car
a Wildcat we call it dread
and we're running
the white line running
in the red Jimmy's got
a bottle and a honey
just waiting to get bred
we drive so fast
there's no town left
and we're headed for
the curve I'm slunk down
on the passenger side
trying to down the velvet
Grady's got a smoke
it's a roll your own
he's blowing smoke fantastic
he grabs another gear
we slosh some Everclear
and the road begins sloping
Jimmy says we're here
and everything disappears
and I'm alone trying to
down the velvet

Mary said there he goes again
Annette said surely
Rose said maybe this time
he'll finish what he started
we can only hope said Mary
oh it's true said Annette
anyone with a rope that big
has got to finish what they've
started you'd know said Rose
I want to know said Mary
big said Annette with lots of
veins not my cup of tea
said Rose pulling up her pants
after pissing I bet you'd need
a bucket said Mary wiping
herself with a clutch of weeds
I guess you'll never find
out said Annette now that
he's climbed the watertower

When Jimmy told people
he could fly nobody came
so when he let loose
his rope he was alone
but all night long
over the roofs of the
trailercourt people
could hear him calling
get out of bed you
motherfuckers I'm
Harry fucking Houdini
and I can fly

When we cut the rope
I looked at Jimmy's face chromatic
asked him if he could breathe better now
he said my throat's a bit dry a little scratchy
I looked at the burst vessels in his eyes
asked if the world stayed dark
he said I could see more than you ever imagined
I said Jimmy you pissed yourself
I said you kicked off
one a your boots and he said
I was dancing the half-breed fancy
like you ain't never seen, dawg

Ligatures of November
burn in the shine
which is their translation
into god chromatic
the beginning of tomorrow
of some common sign
because I am something
here where the roaring is
swaying grateful for the flame
the flourishing we are
calling to   to belong

He sat just out of the shade
out of range of the front doors
of Montgomery Ward where cool air
mixed with the sound from outside
speakers playing music for elevated
people no not no Vietnam vet
Jimmy and I each had a nickel
we knew there was nothing in the store
we could buy except a piece of
hard stale gum from the Lions Club
machine just inside the door so we
started looking through the
pencils he was selling from a
beer can painted red white and deep blue
Jimmy wanted the thick green one
but it was 15 cents I liked the blue one
because it was sharpened the best
the man kept his hands on the sidewalk
hands folded between what was left
of his legs the back of his shaved head
raw and glistening in the sun
his face sagged a bit as if he were
sleeping and there was a cardboard sign
beside him that said God Bless America
just then momma came out and grabbed us
by the hair and pulled us into the store
saying if I ever catch you staring
at one of those dirty people again
I'll snatch you bald-headed
later Jimmy said I bet he was a real
good dancer I bet he was smooth
had moves like glass and made all
the pretty girls swoon

[chorus]

November Echo to Charlie Kilo over
this is Charlie Kilo go ahead November Echo over
what is your ETA Charlie Kilo it seems we've
come upon a pecker wrecker on the way to the ball over
copy that November Echo you are delayed to the dropzone
affirmative Charlie Kilo we will proceed to plan B
and circle the watertower over roger that Charlie Kilo
we will continue screwing the pooch over
the coast is clear for god I repeat the coast is clear
for god over god is on the tower over
copy that Charlie Kilo over we're tightening the noose
everyone the pope is on the rope over everybody switch
to the frequency of flame over let that baby shine
November Echo let that baby shine over copy that Charlie Kilo
all prayers are where they belong over copy that
we will hover the dropzone let's let this fucker hang

Falling snow begins to shine
November Jimmy tucked into
the ground Joe Grady flame
I take a selfie at the watertower
the warning light strobing
and I think about god how
untranslatable his actions are
to the yearnings of our
little moments when we sway
grateful to feel it all
tomorrow and when we return to the
beginning of our calling
and remember the flourishings
and write them in a book
we say home is what is granted
and yet I am here
in the methed-out ghost-town
to which our childhoods
will always belong

November 11th, 2013-December 11th, 2013

RECENT TITLES FROM ALICE JAMES BOOKS

Ghost, like a Place, Iain Haley Pollock

Isako Isako, Mia Ayumi Malhotra

Of Marriage, Nicole Cooley

The English Boat, Donald Revell

We, the Almighty Fires, Anna Rose Welch

DiVida, Monica A. Hand

pray me stay eager, Ellen Doré Watson

Some Say the Lark, Jennifer Chang

Calling a Wolf a Wolf, Kaveh Akbar

We're On: A June Jordan Reader, Edited by Christoph Keller and Jan Heller Levi

Daylily Called It a Dangerous Moment, Alessandra Lynch

Surgical Wing, Kristin Robertson

The Blessing of Dark Water, Elizabeth Lyons

Reaper, Jill McDonough

Madwoman, Shara McCallum

Contradictions in the Design, Matthew Olzmann

House of Water, Matthew Nienow

World of Made and Unmade, Jane Mead

Driving without a License, Janine Joseph

The Big Book of Exit Strategies, Jamaal May

play dead, francine j. harris

Thief in the Interior, Phillip B. Williams

Second Empire, Richie Hofmann

Drought-Adapted Vine, Donald Revell

Refuge/es, Michael Broek

O'Nights, Cecily Parks

Yearling, Lo Kwa Mei-en

Sand Opera, Philip Metres

Devil, Dear, Mary Ann McFadden

Eros Is More, Juan Antonio González Iglesias, Translated by Curtis Bauer

Alice James Books has been publishing poetry since 1973. The press was founded in Boston, Massachusetts as a cooperative wherein authors performed the day-to-day undertakings of the press. This collaborative element remains viable even today, as authors who publish with the press are also invited to become members of the editorial board and participate in editorial decisions at the press. The editorial board selects manuscripts for publication via the press's annual, national competition, the Alice James Award. AJB remains committed to its founders' original mission to support women poets, while expanding upon the scope to include poets of all genders, backgrounds, and stages of their careers. In keeping with our efforts to foster equity and inclusivity in publishing and the literary arts, AJB seeks out poets whose writing possesses the range, depth, and ability to cultivate empathy in our world and to dynamically push against silence. The press was named for Alice James, sister to William and Henry, whose extraordinary gift for writing went unrecognized during her lifetime.

Designed by Anna Reich Design
annareichdesign.com

Printed by McNaughton & Gunn